Discarded

One Mother's Journey with a Psychopath

Indie Mom

DISCLAIMER

I have tried to recreate events from my memories of them. In order to maintain their anonymity in all instances, I have not used actual names of individuals or places. In addition, I may have changed some identifying characteristics and details such as physical properties, occupations and places of residence.

Copyright © 2014 Authored Indie Mom
All rights reserved.

ISBN: 149951851X
ISBN 13: 9781499518511
Library of Congress Control Number: 2014908999
CreateSpace Independent Publishing Platform, North Charleston, SC

Indie Mom

Author Indie Mom is an independent mother of three children. In her professional life, she has worked for twenty-five years with at-risk youth, as well as those with mental, physical, and intellectual disabilities. A personal survivor of domestic abuse, the author shares her story of overcoming damage wrought by a husband with a personality disorder.

WEBSITE
www.discardedindiemom.com

EMAIL
discardedindiemom@gmail.com

DEDICATION

This book is dedicated to three of my personal heroes. Because I had the privilege of watching your gallant efforts in enduring the storm of family dysfunction, I was able to grow up strong and independent as a person and your mother. Thank you, my sons.

And to my dear and cherished anonymous online friends whom I met, and have had the privilege of working with, this past year. Because of you, I have been able to safely tell my story as many times and in as many ways as I needed. This book would not have happened without your support. Thank you: An Old-Fashioned Girl, Barberable, HealingJourney, Indie917, Iris, MorningAfter, Outoftheashes, Peace, Peru, Questionmark, Rydia, SearchingForSunshine, Smitten Kitten and Victoria.

CONTENTS

1
FOREWARD
The Protector

3
INTRODUCTION
Love Never Fails

6
Chapter One
I SEE YOU
The Man Behind the Mask

11
Chapter Two
YOU'LL BE FINE IN FIVE YEARS
Family Law

18
Chapter Three
BROKEN
Pieces of Shattered Lives

27
Chapter Four
OVER THE HILLS AND THROUGH THE WOODS
Father-of-the-Year

35
Chapter Five
ON FINDING A TRIBE
People Who Cared Enough

42
Chapter Six
HERE COMES THE SUN
Recovery and Beyond

48
AFTERWARD
When All is Said and Done

> Parents, however old they and we may grow to be,
> among other things to shield us
> from a sense of our doom.
> As long as they are around,
> we can avoid the fact of our mortality;
> we can still be innocent children.
>
> ~Jane Howard

FOREWARD
The Protector

Psychopaths seek to destroy innocence—trust, love, and childlike wonder. So many of us fear that we've lost these qualities after an abusive encounter, but the healing process is all about discovering that certain things cannot be destroyed. We learn to protect ourselves by forming boundaries, developing self-respect, and building a strong set of values.

But what about those who cannot protect themselves?

How is a child expected to cope with the mind games, manipulation, psychological—and sometimes physical—abuse of a psychopath? It takes a certain amount of resilience from the child, but above all, it takes the love of another human being to shield and protect them from such darkness. Parents dealing with a psychopathic partner must take on so many roles: advocate, fighter, provider, caregiver, mediator, role model, and protector—all the while attempting to heal their own hearts from this unimaginable abuse. The traditional advice of "No Contact" cannot apply when you have children with a toxic individual. They turn your life into a constant state of uncertainty, using your unconditional love as a tool to gain power.

In a custody battle, a psychopath will fight you on every level at every turn, simply because they need to win. Always. They treat everything in life as a game they need to win, including their children. It isn't because they genuinely love them or care about their welfare. They don't even really want the responsibility of raising them. To a psychopath, children are nothing more than possessions or property to be "won" like any other marital asset in the divorce. While you are literally fighting for your life and the lives of your children, the psychopathic parent will be using them as pawns in their sadistic game to further control and cause you more pain.

Despite all of that, you must remain the voice of reason and consistency for your child. You must somehow absorb and deflect the toxic, hypocritical garbage being thrown at every moment in order to protect your child's innocence. You must ignore the projection, gaslighting, and smear campaign being used as weapons against you and your credibility. You must somehow put your own hopes, dreams, and healing on hold, in order to fight this war that's been declared on your family with dignity and grace.

Indie Mom tells the story of this battle in heartbreaking detail, offering invaluable bits of wisdom and hope along the way. She provides the knowledge and gentle validation that every parent needs in order to protect their children during the difficult path toward long-term freedom. And despite an overwhelming journey of her own, she has still dedicated countless hours helping other families survive this nightmare.

Indie Mom is a true protector, in every sense of the word, and her story will change the world.

Smitten Kitten & Peace
PsychopathFree.com

> In the flush of love's light
> we dare to be brave
> And suddenly we see
> that love costs all we are
> and will ever be.
> Yet, it is only love
> which sets us free.
>
> ~Maya Angelou

INTRODUCTION
Love Never Fails

It goes without saying that those of us who share custody with a personality-disordered parent can find ourselves living a special kind of hell. While trying to manage our mental and physical health from an unhealthy marriage or relationship, we have the task of caring for the needs of our most precious children. It is a daunting road to travel. Our world is made up of court dates, lawyers, divorce teams, therapists, judges and others who have the ability to control our lives with little to no understanding of the toxic person on the other side of the table. We experience a loss of control and question our sanity while living on adrenaline. There are sleepless nights, physical ailments and just a whole lot of noise. For some of us it seems like an insurmountable mountain to climb while for others it's like being at the bottom of a deep, dark pit with no light ahead as we find ourselves living the catchphrase one step forward, two steps back.

How can parents survive this? How can parents simultaneously care for themselves, manage the onslaught of a seemingly deranged person's wrath, and be there for innocent children who need and deserve so much from life? What battles are worth fighting? What, if anything, is in the power of parents facing these challenges?

I believed wholeheartedly at one time that my needs, and the needs of my children, would be met through family law services that I had began to rely upon for help when I filed for divorce. It was a painful realization that it would be financially impossible to get the help I thought I deserved in caring for my children and self. I learned that once engaged with all of the players involved in marriage dissolution and child custody, the battles were endless. And during the battles, the needs of the children seemed to be the last thing that was ever addressed. I was starring in some kind of horror show, and I knew that if I didn't get out I would die. Literally. I was losing my mind, on the verge of losing my job, and my physical health was failing. It was the thought of my children not having me in their lives that stopped me in my tracks. I made the decision to disengage by turning my back to lawyers and the legal system. I began to navigate independently through unfamiliar and frightening territory. The love for my children became the most powerful source I needed in taking control of my life, embracing our family, and arriving at a place I never imagined existed.

My healing journey began when an old friend suggested I find a twelve-step support group due to my belief that the demise of my marriage was my husband's alcohol abuse. Within this support group of complete strangers, I began to share tidbits of my life's story. That experience led me to a local women's abuse group. While listening to their stories and sharing my own, I knew I was not alone. I then found a personal therapist and with her persistent and gentle guidance, I took apart my relationship with my husband piece by piece. I was reclaiming my personhood.

During these times, I also read. And read and read. It felt as though the floodgates of my psyche were thrust open. And then I found a very safe and accepting abuse recovery forum where I could advance in my healing journey by integrating what I had learned from support groups and counseling, and telling my story as many times and in as many ways as I needed. I was moving and arranging all of the pieces of my puzzling life. When I was finally able to stand back and take a look at what it really had been about, I saw a beautiful and compassionate woman who endured the wrath of an angry and controlling man for most of her life. And sadly, I also saw three innocent and beautiful children who were gravely affected by the chronic mistreatment of their mother at the hands of their father.

If you are reading this book it's most likely because you believe your life, and the lives of your children, are being impacted by a toxic parent. You are not alone. I have read hundreds of stories of parents and families just like mine who struggle to make sense of the hell they are living. My story does not contain all the answers. It does not call upon any one researched theory, nor does it cite experts in the field of family law, child psychiatry or social services. It defines my journey through a labyrinth of internal conflict created by a psychopath. This journey is fueled by a fierce love for my children beating steadily and deeply within my heart.

I cannot begin to express how sorry I am for your pain, yet it is my greatest hope that you find the courage and strength you need in these pages to stand a little taller, think a little more clearly and realize without a doubt that a parent's love never fails. It is the constant that you need to return to again and again as you commit to rebuilding your life and the lives of your children.

Indie Mom
May 15, 2014

> I used to think the worst thing in life
> was to end up all alone, it's not.
> The worst thing in life is to end up
> with people that make you feel all alone.
>
> ~Robin Williams

Chapter One
I SEE YOU
The Man Behind the Mask

If anyone had told me during our life together that I was married to a psychopath, I would have thought they were delusional. Psychopaths are deranged killers. My husband was simply a very complicated man who was difficult to live with. We had met in college. I had no idea then of the characteristics I was looking for in a partner, yet I saw qualities in him that I admired and that drew me to him romantically. He was sensitive, kind, gentle and had a sense of humor. He was a physically beautiful man, charismatic and confident. Wherever he went people stopped to talk to him or call out to him. The immediate and sincere compliments that began shortly after we met focused on my appearance, my voice, the way I walked, and the way I listened and offered unconditional support for his endless woes that no one else understood. It was as if I was on a euphoric drug.

That's the only way I could describe the feeling I was experiencing. We liked the same foods, shared a favorite color, listened to the same music and liked to spend time alone and away from the noise of life. Within a few months of getting to know one another, and spending every moment we could together, he announced that he truly believed he had found his soul mate. He was perfect and I could hardly believe I was deserving of this amazing man. We moved in together within six months, were married four years after that, and would spend a total of almost thirty years together.

~~~~~

The disagreements between us started out as simple tiffs that were easily forgotten, yet our arguments would escalate in severity throughout the years. He was quick to anger yet could switch it off at any time and resume a calm, seemingly controlled demeanor almost as if he had two personalities competing with one another. Verbal arguments met with physicality as the years passed, from hovering over me and resuming close proximity with occasional chest poking to being pushed down onto a cement floor nine months pregnant with our youngest child when he stumbled toward me in a drunken rage. Toward the end of our marriage, he began calling me the most vile names I had ever heard while clenching his fists at his side or raising them up toward me. Always I would try to shield the children from any sign of discord as this mistreatment occurred in the privacy of our home.

As horrid as it sounds, his gentle and loving and kind side was perfectly opposite. I basked in his assuredness that I was his soul mate, that we were a perfect fit, that he would always care for me, that I was a beautiful woman and an amazing mother. The accolades he would mostly bestow upon me in public, to our mutual colleagues, friends, family and our children made me feel on top of the world. There were always flowers, little gifts or a special look or tilt of the head with a smile after our hard times. In the beginning of our life together, this gentle and loving side was more frequent and lasted longer than his anger and silence, yet year by year the gentle man was harder to find and the cruel man more and more present. Through it all I remained committed to our marriage, and caring for and loving our children. My internal mantra was the wedding vow that called for better or worse. I convinced myself to believe the worse times were more frequent due to life's stresses and my shortcomings. I truly believed that in time we'd experience the 'for better' part. I lived for the realization of that promise.

Early into our marriage and careers, we accepted jobs overseas. Our lifestyle allowed us to live very comfortably, to travel and to save money. Within a few years we started our family. To our international circle of colleagues and friends, my husband was the devout family man and a person of faith. We had a beautiful little home and three perfect little boys. We had great jobs, had made some fun friends and visited our families back home during our vacation times. I believed that we were living the 'for better' part of our married life, and I felt truly at peace. It wasn't to last. Unbeknownst to me, my husband had become known for binge drinking, womanizing with married women and female colleagues, and expressing his anger towards people who would disagree with him or question him on his behaviors. All I knew was that at home he was becoming more and more sullen and argumentative, giving me the silent treatment for long periods of time. I lived on as if no one else but me was aware of any of this. I was making excuses for him and covering up for his drinking and the irresponsible behaviors that put his family in harm's way in a foreign country. Friends fell to the wayside and I began to live a very isolated life from anyone who could help or offer support to a young mother and distressed wife. We were eventually asked to resign from our jobs.

Leaving the international lifestyle was devastating for me. We had been abroad for ten years. Our small and protected community was ideal for raising a young family. Food was inexpensive. Our housing and car were provided through the company. I had a nanny at my disposal as well as a housekeeper. Our sons loved their school and little friends. These were the realities I had clung to while living in denial of my husband's gradual demise. In my mind, we were going to live overseas until our sons graduated from high school.

It was at the health club swimming pool surrounded by my children and others that my husband told me we both had lost our jobs. I have a picture of my elementary aged sons holding their toddler brother in the water that I had taken just moments before I heard the news. I have lost track of how many times I've looked at that picture. For me, it marks the end of their innocence. My husband blamed our firing on someone who must have had a vendetta against him, as the chief executive officer reviewed with him the history of his unhealthy and toxic behaviors. He vehemently denied these accusations while shifting an emphasis onto my behaviors. According to him, the professional community saw me as a very ill woman with severe personality disorders. Taking care of me was impacting his ability to do his job. That's why we had to leave. Within six weeks we packed up our lives while neighbors, colleagues and friends kept their distance. The gossip turned scandalous.

We moved back to the USA to be near our families, and my husband kept the meme alive that this was an opportunity for us to start a whole new life. One of his female friends from the community we had just left had helped him create a list of mental health professionals within our new town for his deranged wife. It wasn't difficult to relocate and acclimatize to the states. We found jobs, bought a home, enrolled our kids in school, and soon had a new circle of friends; however, it took only a couple of years for the same pattern of behaviors to begin to wear me down. There would be new behaviors, too, that I started to see in my husband – mainly his perception of women. When I'd vent or discuss anything about my work or the children's days, he would reference female colleagues who were 'cunts' or 'whiny bitches' and that he didn't want to deal with this when he came home to me. I began to focus more and more on the children's busy lives, my work and our beautiful home. He in turn worked longer hours trying to advance to more lucrative positions. And the years continued to pass.

It was when our oldest sons had just started high school, and our youngest was in elementary school, that I discovered my husband was having an affair with a fellow colleague. I started to experience flashbacks from our life abroad as I felt myself reliving the last time my security was threatened. Contrite yet also somewhat smug, my husband agreed to attend marriage counseling. For the next several weeks he stayed in the home. I begged him to stop the affair. I ramped up my accommodating, kind and loving persona. Discussion after discussion focused on his happiness and how he needed to make a change in his life. We had painful conversations about the other woman and what she offered to him that I could not. I talked about our sons and how their lives were going to be negatively impacted if we ended our marriage.

He agreed to marriage counseling, so we worked with our separate therapists, who were a husband-wife team, suggesting we start that way and then eventually come together. We made our own appointments. It was at one, and the last, of my sessions that I realized my husband was in the adjoining office with his therapist. In a moment of silence between my therapist and me, I heard his voice through the wall loudly proclaim that I was crazy to believe he'd ever leave the other woman. Later when I made my discovery known to him, he accused the husband-wife therapist team of setting up the scenario in order to side with me that he stay in the marriage. About a week later, I demanded he leave our home and I filed for divorce. I sensed an immediate relief. He was gone. I thought that the hell I had been living was over. I couldn't have been more mistaken.

> Your life is always talking to you.
> But are you paying attention?
> Are you paying attention to the circumstances,
> situation – and yes, even the people – who support
> you in being less than and doing less than
> you know you're capable of doing?
> Because if you're not paying attention,
> you'll surround yourself with things and people
> that don't have your best interests at heart.
>
> ~Iyanla Vanzant

Chapter Two
YOU'LL BE FINE IN FIVE YEARS
Family Law

I chose my divorce lawyer on a recommendation from a good friend who worked in the legal profession. She knew of this lawyer's work and said he was a kind and fair man and that he was known as the best trial attorney in town. I paid the fee for a thirty minute consult and sobbed my way through the initial questioning. Handing me a box of tissues he began the asking. What did I do for living? What did my husband do for a living? How long had we been married? How many children did we have? What kind of father was he? Did I think he was having an affair? Was I having an affair? And there were endless questions about assets, debts and savings. I didn't know at the time that this consult was also a risk assessment for the lawyer. How lengthy of a case was this going to be? Did I have the financial resources to carry the case to closure? Would I be a difficult client?

It was all so disconcerting, and I couldn't put my finger on the reason for my unsettled feelings. I was waiting to hear that my husband was going to be held accountable for the mistreatment of our children and me. I wanted to leave the office believing that he was going to be in real trouble, justice would be served, and he would be punished.

Traumatized and searching for help, an attorney's office shouldn't have been my first stop. The lawyer recommended I take some time to think things through. He commented that I appeared pretty beaten down and handed me a business card of a good therapist he knew. I stopped at the front desk on the way out and asked about going forth. I didn't even know what a retainer was. I asked if this was the cost of the entire divorce. She replied that it was dependent on how complicated things would get throughout the process. I wondered about that comment for a long time after leaving the office. It was a big step for me to even schedule this initial meeting. It meant to me that I was considering ending my marriage. I was frightened. The one person I sought for reassurance and approval in my life wouldn't be able to help me make a decision. I couldn't talk about the divorce attorney with my husband.

I met up with my friend who recommended the lawyer to get her input. She explained a retainer, how attorneys bill for services, and how much other couples she knew had spent on divorces. She nonchalantly commented that the expense and difficulty of a divorce was the main reason she hadn't already filed. She just wasn't ready for such a major life change. Over a glass of wine and sharing stories of our husbands' moods and our sons' school activities, I decided against filing for divorce that day; however, I was to return to the attorney's office four months later. I had just thrown my husband out of the house.

~~~~~

The paralegal assigned to my case was kind, compassionate and savvy. I liked her. She played on my emotions by addressing what I wanted to hear months ago from the attorney. She passionately agreed with me that my husband was a cruel man, that she would take care of me, and that he'd get his in the end. We discussed the most important things that I wanted from the divorce, and I told her custody of my children and the family home. I shared the recent fight with my husband when I had threatened him with divorce and taking our children if he didn't leave the other woman. His reply to that threat was that I could have the children, as he never wanted them anyway. And since he hadn't spoken to our two oldest since he left the family home, I was fairly certain, I told her, that he wouldn't cause problems where the children were concerned. He was also about to inherit the family estate from his deceased parents. I was fairly certain he wouldn't fight over our house either. The paralegal told me that I was probably right on both accounts, yet that divorces can get ugly and people can seemingly lose their minds over the simplest of things. I was adamant, though, that I wanted a civil divorce and there was to be no mudslinging. She laughed. I was told the temporary orders would be presented to the judge, and that they were to be looked at as the guidelines my husband and I would follow regarding the children, finances and the home pending the final divorce.

I arrived to the courthouse looking like hell. I hadn't been eating or sleeping well since my husband had left, and the black dress I decided to wear looked two sizes too big. My face was blotchy from crying and my eyes swollen. The lawyer and I found each other in the hallway amidst other divorcees and attorneys. He took one look at me and firmly advised me to go to the ladies room and pull myself to together. When I returned, I was told to stand next to him when we approached the judge, show no emotion, make no sounds, and to refrain from looking at my husband or his lawyer. As both lawyers bantered back and forth talking about living arrangements, finances, custody of the children and visitation schedules, I stood shaking. I had never been inside a courtroom, aside from jury duty, and it was difficult to take it all in while listening to complete strangers talk openly about what I considered the most private of matters between my husband and me.

Our full names rang out along with the names and ages of our children, our place of employment, salaries, checking account balances, health care companies, mortgage payments, makes and models of our cars and on and on. At one point I heard snickers coming from the divorcees waiting to be called and I was embarrassed. Then I heard my husband's lawyer state that he would ultimately like shared custody yet was in agreement at that time that the mother assume the primary custodial role with a standard visitation schedule of every-other-weekends and holidays while he took some time to secure a suitable place to live for the children and himself. I audibly sucked in my breath and felt hot tears welling in my eyes. My lawyer leaned over and whispered in my ear to stop showing emotion.

The court appearance was over in a matter of fifteen minutes. I would rarely see my attorney after that. I was told to return to his office where the paralegal would fully review the temporary orders the judge had just signed to make sure I understood everything. I was still shaking. I had no idea how I was going to care for our three children and the home while working full time, and survive off of my income and the calculated child support. She reminded me what we discussed in our first session together – that no one party is going to walk away rich and the other poor. It was about dividing one household into two, and that is never a win-win. She wished me well and said to go home and rest. Everything would settle down now as we took time to adjust to the temporary orders.

What ensued for the next eighteen months was a high conflict divorce that would portray me as an unstable, untruthful, unfaithful and selfish woman, and he a battered husband who bravely chose to leave an abusive marriage. I was irresponsible with money, inattentive to the needs of our children, and consumed with my career. Court documents, sworn statements and rebuttals would focus on him and how difficult his life had been with a woman like me. And apparently he had wanted out of our marriage for years, knew that I was emotionally and physically unavailable, and had no other choice but to seek companionship elsewhere. There was little to no regard for the children within his filed documents, yet he would frequently text or call begging me to help him reconnect with our oldest sons whom he still hadn't spoken to, so he could tell them his side of the story. When I replied that it was up to him to reach out to our sons and attempt to reconcile, I would receive a letter from his lawyer a few days later accusing me of poisoning our children against him.

I could see no point to any of this. He now had everything he said he wanted. He was gone from our home and marriage. The children he said that I could have prior to leaving our home were no longer in his life. He had a doting new lover, and was about to become financially secure for the rest of his life. Yet here he was continuing to abuse me through the guises of family law.

I had little time for self-care or finding any kind of professional support for my intense distress, increased anxiety and hyper-vigilance. I felt alienated and alone, angry and irritable, jumpy and easily startled. My friends and family were burning out with the endless drama. Colleagues were kind and comforting, yet I knew it was inappropriate to continue to bring my personal woes into the workplace. I would end up spending thousands of dollars in legal fees. I would unnecessarily call my lawyer trying to defend myself against the onslaught of false allegations and other issues I thought were relevant. I demanded he write letters for this or that and expected him to act like my personal therapist. Once there was a forty-five minute telephone conversation during which he was very comforting and solved a problem I had unnecessarily created. It felt wonderful to be heard, until I received the bill. The co-pay for a therapist would have been ten times less expensive. I'd continue to schedule pointless meetings with the paralegal to inquire about why things weren't moving along more quickly than I thought they should.

It became apparent that my husband was not interested in joint custody. He continued his silent treatment with our oldest sons, and was not exercising many of the visits with our youngest that were laid out in the temporary parenting plan. He had all but removed himself from his former life. My lawyer considered this a huge gain for me, yet all I saw was a father who abandoned his own children. I meticulously documented everything my husband was doing, assuming he was going to be held accountable for the pain he was causing. I was hoping he would feel guilty for his absenteeism in our lives by regularly sending certified mail containing spreadsheets of expenses I had accrued of the children's extra-curricular activities, synopsis of doctor appointments, school calendars and schedules, and even a journal of how they were each behaving since he left. My efforts were met with silence and most of the certified letters would be returned to me unclaimed. My lawyer sat me down and told me to just stop and that in no uncertain terms was a judge going to hold him accountable for the lifestyle he was currently living, how he chose to leave our marriage, and his decisions to not be in our children's lives. He encouraged me to begin to accept these realities as no amount or method of 'begging' on my part was going to change things. I knew then that my sons' needs and rights to be heard would continue to be ignored, while the lawyers focused instead on keeping conflict high between the divorcing parents.

Eventually my lawyer scheduled a mediation session to address the outstanding issues needing to be resolved pending issuance of a divorce decree and final orders. There were disagreements on child support and spousal maintenance, a few possessions, and the appraisal price of the family home. The mediation session lasted six hours. We were in separate rooms with our perspective lawyers while the mediator went back and forth with messages of agreement or disagreement in what each had offered. At the end of the day, only the price of the home remained unsettled. It was in my best interest to get the lowest appraisal possible since I would have to compensate my husband his share of the equity as part of the divorce settlement. My husband would not agree to the lower appraisal. I heard him speaking loudly and angrily to his lawyer and mediator, a door slam and then his car speed away. My lawyer informed me that we had no other options than trial as a judge would now have to decide. I was once again told that I needed to face some realities. My financial situation was going to drastically change. I was most likely going to be an independent parent, and I may want to think about selling the home and cutting my losses. I was to start planning for my future and rebuilding my life.

'You'll be fine in five years ...' were the last words I heard. And then I did the one thing that I learned is a cardinal sin in family law when represented by a trial attorney. After leaving the mediation session, I attempted to communicate with my husband with bargains towards a settlement. He would not respond, yet his lawyer passed on the information to mine. Weeks went by before I received a letter in the mail that my lawyer was withdrawing from my case. He wished me well yet felt that I needed to find a lawyer with whom I could be happy.

With the encouragement of friends and family, and because I didn't want to spend any more money on legal fees, I decided to go forth by representing myself. I learned it was called pro se. My friend in the legal profession told me not to do it. With the trial date having been set, I spent weeks learning to complete paperwork correctly and reading the handbook about court rules and procedures that was provided to me by the court facilitator. I had no idea what I was doing. The day of the hearing, and in the courtroom, my husband's lawyer informed the judge that she believed we could reach a settlement without a trial. The lower home appraisal was acceptable to her client after all. We reviewed the final orders which were nearly identical to the temporary orders issued eighteen months earlier. She would draw up the final orders for presentation in two weeks.

Upon the advice of my friend in the legal profession, I sought out and hired a second lawyer to look over the final orders prior to the judge signing. I had already verbally agreed to these orders in the courtroom so there was very little this new lawyer could do, aside from addressing the parenting plan that he said was vague in certain areas and still open for some discussion. I spent a good amount of time with him sharing how my children's father had violated the parenting plan and how manipulative he had been the past many months. This lawyer ended up accompanying me to court where he successfully argued for some changes that would neutralize many of the behaviors that kept both of us engaged with conflict. The plan stated that our older children could decide their own visitation, yet my former husband's lawyer had also written up a travel plan regarding visitation logistics for our youngest. His father was moving three hours away. This was the first time I was to hear of this and I was in shock. I was now going to have to drive six hours total every other weekend for exchange of our child. With the divorce finalized and a solid parenting plan in place, I wanted to feel free. I wanted it to be over and to begin my new life. I left the courthouse feeling defeated and as if my former husband was still in control of my life.

What transpired following the final divorce was beyond anything I could have imagined. The father of my sons would now turn his attention and energy toward our oldest two whom he believed were betraying him with their silence regarding his decision to leave our home and seek personal happiness. Not only would he marry the other woman, he would begin to systematically engage in parental and sibling alienation. Our oldest sons would end up even more angry and shut off, while our youngest endured a position that demanded alliance to his father's new wife and him. This hell would last for three years.

> Let the hard things in life break you.
> Let them effect you.
> Let them change you.
> Let these hard moments inform you.
> Let this pain be your teacher.
> What is the lesson in this wind?
> What is this storm trying to tell you?
> What will you learn if you face it with courage?
>
> ~Pema Chodron

Chapter Three
BROKEN
Pieces of Shattered Lives

I don't know the exact amount of time my husband had been having an affair before I found out. I predict it began long before my initial consultation visit to the divorce attorney when our fighting began to escalate and I sensed a gradual shift in his personality. He was raging more frequently. He was storming out of the house on a moment's notice only to return happy, calm and as if nothing had happened several hours earlier. When he was gone from home or not at work, he wouldn't answer his phone for hours on end, even when there were urgent issues with our children. Yet he was sending me flowers at work, sweet texts asking if I was thinking about him, and special gifts for our sons for no apparent reason. Then bizarrely, and for the first time in our marriage, he bought himself new jeans and underwear and changed his standard cologne.

At the same time, he had begun questioning me on every cent I spent as opposed to giving me free reign with our family finances as he had for the past thirty some years. He started to talk about having his own money to spend on the things he wanted, and that he also wanted to learn more about balancing the budget I had been so good at.

Then one day he came home and informed me that he had opened his own checking account into which he would begin depositing his paycheck. I was to continue to pay the bills from my account, as usual, and then let him know balances so that he could reimburse me exactly half of the monthly expenses. If I needed anything extra for the children, I was to discuss it with him first and that we'd have to come to an agreement on the importance of whatever it was. I could not wrap my head around this. He brought home two-thirds of the money needed to maintain our home and family. Yet I was now to pay half of these expenses. I felt a fear like no other that day he stood above me for almost an hour badgering and yelling as I went through spreadsheets and monthly budgets showing every penny I spent and on what.

The documents and financial disclosures he had to provide my attorney when I filed for divorce some months later would confirm he was wining and dining another woman all along. While I had been spending time and energy on re-budgeting our family finances and enduring his rages when I asked for anything above my fifty percent, he was taking another woman out for drinks and dinner, hooking up in hotels, and buying perfume and lingerie.

~~~~~

No matter what the circumstances had been within our marriage and life, never had I felt so violated when I discovered the affair. I had found my husband talking on his phone in our garage on Christmas Eve night. I don't even know why I went looking for him, yet when I heard his voice I stopped and just listened. Something didn't sound right. I felt sick when I realized that I was eavesdropping on a romantic and sexually charged conversation. It took me about a minute before I made my presence known and began yelling at him to get off the phone. He assured the woman on the other end that all was well and he'd call later. He then tried to deny what I had heard and claimed I was crazy. He was just speaking to a friend and I needed to check my attitude before accusing him of anything. I had no right. At nine-o-clock in the evening, and with our children in the house getting ready for bed in anticipation of Christmas morning, he got in his truck and drove off. I put the boys to bed, arranged all of their presents under the tree, and sat in the dark staring at the lights through big, hot tears that wouldn't stop. He returned home at two-o-clock in the morning telling me he had been sitting in the park thinking.

My life as I had known it was shattered. What transpired after that night can only be described as a traumatized wife begging the abuser to remain in her life. There would be endless discussions, fights, ultimatums and justifications either in our cars, in the garage or when the children were gone from home. I would call him frequently asking him where he was. When he'd leave I'd ask where he was going. When he agreed to attend marriage counseling prior to either one of us filing for divorce, I thought this was a good sign we could begin to repair whatever it was that was broken. After several weeks, he agreed to end the affair on the condition he could remain friends with the other woman. She had come from an abusive marriage, after all, and was a fragile and kind person who would always need his help. He suggested that a trial separation between the two of us was probably best and that he had already decided he would be moving out the following week. I felt nothing but anger as I threatened to divorce him and take our children. He replied that he didn't want them anyway. I was numb.

A few days later we sat the children down to tell them that their father was moving out of our home. He did all of the talking as our sons began to cry. There was no mention of another woman, only that I was ill and him staying in the home was making me sicker. Then he got up and left the room. I followed him and asked if that was all he had to say. Silence. What happened next is what I will forever regret with regards to how I handled him physically leaving our home. I demanded he leave that minute. I gathered duffle bags and started frantically packing his clothes while he took the children into another part of the house. I hauled what I had packed to the front door and onto the steps. I tried with all my might to throw some of it into the yard. He stood watching, chuckled and calmly asked if the drama was necessary. I used a few choice words while letting the neighborhood know what it looked like to throw a cheater out on the street. Doors were slammed and he was gone. The children heard and saw it all. Their father never returned.

It was as if a tornado struck down and left in its wake piles of rubble that was once our life. It took me a very long time to understand that what would happen to all of us would not be the direct result of my husband leaving that night. It took a long time for me to set down the guilt I felt for the pain my sons endured. For years I had lied for him, preached his goodness to all who would listen, stood by his side when he lost jobs, our home, our friends, apologized to school teachers and administrators when he would rage in meetings about our sons misbehaviors, laughed off his hurtful sarcasm toward my sisters and female friends, and turned away when I saw his friendly advances toward other women. And together we lived inside a bubble of dysfunction where we kept our children and selves exposed to never ending cycles of calmness and complete disarray.

When my sons were little they use to admire a set of tiny, little pretty clay pots I had found on our travels abroad. I would use an analogy with them ever so often that we were all like those little clay pots. Each was unique and created with care to be admired but then set down carefully so as not to break. Over the years, and inevitably, lots of little cracks had emerged within my sons and me. My husband's physical abandonment was just the pivotal event that nudged each of us with the right amount of force to start breaking apart the pieces.

It was not easy to ask for help in parenting abandoned children. The one person I wanted and thought I needed left me sitting amongst the destruction that he was responsible for creating. And even though I considered myself an efficient mother and one who always took the initiative to get things done, a broken family was beyond anything I was capable of fixing. I was a shell of person, and aside from adult siblings and a few friends who were on the receiving end of my emotional breakdowns, I really had no idea who to turn to or what to do.

I was in unbearable pain – for them, for me, for us. In the midst of searching for answers, I can only describe my new relationship with my children as one of a triage nurse. All three of them were a mess and I did what I could in those early days, weeks and months while in shock myself, and trying to work full time. I cooked and cleaned, took them to doctor appointments and therapy sessions, drove them to school and sports practices, helped them with homework, and attended school functions. I was present and accounted for and on autopilot. I knew in my gut, though, that with trauma, crises follow.

Within a few months following his departure, my sons and I would learn about the other woman through a very public and open display of their relationship within a community we had lived in for ten years. My husband would also recruit her to help him in his smear campaign against me. He had left because I was an alcoholic. I neglected our children. I was having an affair. The other woman wasn't a home wrecker because our marriage was over long before she entered the picture. She was introduced to my husband's entire family and they loved her. They were all so happy he had finally found someone to love him for the man he was. He would begin to attend her high school daughter's sporting events, and take her entire family boating on the river where our family had gone for the past ten summers. He'd gift her daughter with the car that belonged to his mother, who recently had passed away, while my two sons and I shared one car. People would see my husband and the other woman at the mall, in grocery stores, and even skiing where he had taken our children for the past many winters. When my husband's father died -- the same man who had been my father for nearly thirty years -- the other woman's name appeared in the obituary along side my husband's and all of his siblings and their spouses. The funeral mass would take place in the same church where my husband and I were married.

When I'd attempt to communicate with him regarding the children those first few months after he'd left, replies became more and more dismissive. He had given me five different phone numbers to reach him. I'd receive a letter from his lawyer to stop contacting him at work, even though it was the only phone that would be answered, or he'd be filing harassment charges. Then there were the texts that he hadn't loved me in twenty years. He was finally at peace. Please leave him alone. He trusted me to take good care of our children. I needed to move on with my life.

What happened to our high school sons over the following three school years, until graduation, is a timeline of events that I don't like to revisit. After all, what mother looks at her beautiful little baby or playful toddler or little league player and visualizes countless school referrals, detentions, suspensions, expulsions and juvenile delinquency? Who dreams of the day she will see her son standing in handcuffs in an orange jump suit in front of a judge instead of going to the high school prom? What mother invites drugs, threats of suicide, and destruction of property into her family and home? Who can imagine living with a vindictive, defiant, angry, stubborn and hostile youth who exhausts a parent to the point of surrender? What mother looks forward to spending afternoons and evenings in endless appointments with pediatricians, psychiatrists, judges or school administrators, or sitting in an emergency room looking at her teenager's beaten and bloodied face? Who is able to predict the day when there are no more hugs or 'I love you, Mom'?

Today my greatest desire is that the people who were outside our lives, yet looking in and in positions to help, could see how their reactions to my teenage sons' crises contributed to a very painful existence instead of toward healing and growth.

First, their father chose to turn his back and walk away from a 'better life' when our house of cards finally came tumbling down. The man my sons sought acceptance from for their entire lives relayed the message that they didn't matter more than his personal happiness. This same man would shower them with praise and accolades in public, yet burn messages into their minds in private from elementary school until the day he left that they were not good enough, that they needed to 'man up', that they were stupid and lazy and didn't know how to work for anything, didn't respect their mother, that they owed everything they had to him for working all day long, and that he couldn't own anything nice because he was spending all his money on his children. How many people in our lives, aside from me, saw this? Who remained silent? And who tried to help? When a boy's father not only parents like this but walks away from the responsibility of fatherhood while simultaneously discarding his mother, what does it do to the child? How is he to make sense of such madness? Who can he turn to for help? The battered and broken mother? What amount of anger can a child hold inside until it can no longer can be contained?

There were others. Their father's adult family members all but disappeared from their life when they did nothing to deserve such contempt and further abandonment. Through their silences, uncles, aunts and their only living grandfather stood beside a man who walked out on his family.

High school administrators and counselors all but ignored my pleas for help, and instead let my sons flounder before they were punished and humiliated in front of their peers. A campus safety officer stalked one of my sons relentlessly until he lived up to her expectations that he was indeed a noncompliant, angry and hostile student. She walked behind us once when he was temporarily expelled. With his friends watching and with her hand on her weapon, she yelled that we were not welcome back and that my son was a disrespectful delinquent. A principal at a new school placed him on a behavioral contract until he proved he could comply with staff members. The contract denied him the ability to play sports. He lost opportunities to interact with coaches and other athletes, and was cut from his traveling tournament team's roster.

A pediatrician and psychiatrist both refused to write a prescription for anxiety and depression when he began to refuse to leave the home because he had disclosed during an intake interview that he smoked pot, and was therefore labeled a drug abuser who needed to come clean before treatment. And there was that police officer in the emergency room telling me, while my son lay bleeding from a blow to the head after a fight, and as if he couldn't hear, that he would likely end up in prison.

For three years all I seemed to be able to do was pray for just one more day. I prayed for one more day to validate my high school sons in any way I could, and with every chance I had, in hopes it would make a difference in the direction their lives were taking. I neglected my health and wellness. I suffered from eczema on my hands, anxiety, panic attacks, episodic anger and insomnia. I would have to take more days off from work than my contract allowed for court hearings and school related issues. I neglected my work and fell behind in projects.

Slowly, and insidiously, they were learning to what extent their father would continue his psychological abuse. Although their father had become independently wealthy through his family inheritance, there would be no extra financial support in helping me with the unexpected expenses of high school and raising young men. Their hobbies and talents could no longer be funded. New sports equipment wasn't affordable, and traveling with tournament teams had to be reconsidered. There were proms and senior pictures I borrowed money for. When I petitioned the courts for help in holding their father accountable for at least drivers' education classes and car insurance, the answer was that basic child support was all he was required to provide.

My oldest sons managed to graduate from their perspective high schools on time and with transcripts that were college ready. Prior to their eighteenth birthday, and when they had made their college decisions, I prepared the court documents to petition their father for what was called post-secondary child support. A custodial parent was required to petition the courts for help from the other parent for educational expenses past high school. It was an arduous task to once again learn how to complete the necessary legal paperwork, schedule a hearing and represent myself in family law court. Rebuttals to my proposed college financial plan were met with the same type of responses that had become standard in our divorce. In what was yet another attempt to wear me down, their father's pages of replies accused me of being irresponsible in encouraging our sons to go off to college. There were implications we had purposely selected expensive universities, that I hadn't involved him in any of the decision-making, and with juvenile records there'd be no guarantee of financial aid. Evidently, according to him, I had allowed them to live carelessly and irresponsibly during their high school years, and therefore this was going to be the same approach they'd have toward a college education. He was reluctant to offer financial support.

I did my best at the two separate hearings in making my case heard, while presenting my former husband's financial profile, in showing he was more than capable of helping provide our sons with a college education of their choosing. It was when his lawyer proceeded, in an open and public courtroom, to refer to me as untruthful, vindictive, and unreasonable – in addition to describing my sons as incapable of obtaining a college degree based on their high school behaviors – that I knew this was just going to be nothing more than another battle orchestrated by her on behalf of my former husband. And if the judge mandated that he help with expenses, did I really want to remain in contact with him for the possibility of four years?

When it was my turn to speak, I faced his lawyer and asked how was it that she could stand in superior court throughout divorce proceedings, and now for child support modifications, and do nothing more than discredit a mother's character who had endured the never-ending onslaught of her client's cruelty while trying to independently raise three traumatized children. And that was it. I set down any bit of hope I still had within me that this man would ever do anything for anyone aside himself. I thanked the judge for her time, dismissed my motion of petition for college support, and walked out of the courtroom.

> Your journey has molded you for the greater good.
> It was exactly what it needed to be.
> Don't think you've lost time.
> It took each and every situation you have encountered
> to bring you to the now.
> And now is right on time.
>
> ~Asha Tyson

Chapter Four
OVER THE HILLS AND THROUGH THE WOODS
Father-of-the-Year

The divorce process took eighteen months while the scandal surrounding my husband's pubic affair within our community and mutual workplace was center stage. Even though my two high school sons stopped communicating with their father the night he left our home, our elementary aged son remained in contact with him primarily through the visitation schedule outlined in the parenting plan. I was the primary custodial parent and my husband the 'every-other-weekend-holiday' father. Along with an outline of a custody division based on the school calendar, there were orders for child support, health insurance, and instructions on how to communicate in the best interests of the children. It was a plan that I would consult frequently for the next three years, at least, as a sort of rulebook in engaging with a manipulative father while managing the lives of three children.

In the first weeks of our separation, and when we were still communicating, I wiped away my husband's tears of sorrow and pain that this is what his life would look like. He wanted me to tell him how he was supposed to live only seeing his sons for this amount of time? Could I please help him to get the older boys to acknowledge him? It was a beautiful, sunny spring day when he had come to our home while the children were gone. We sat on the front porch and I tried to address these questions as well as both of our new roles, where he would live and how we were all going to go forth. There were no easy answers. He seemed heartbroken and sorrowful yet I did not sense remorse of any kind. We hugged for a long time, both crying, before he turned and walked away. There was a moment as I was watching him leave when he turned back to look at me, and with a tilt of his head he offered a slight smile.

~~~~~

Throughout our sons' lives their father had taken an active role. He helped care for them when they were babies, carried them everywhere he went, and starting introducing them to sports from the moment they learned to walk. Mini golf clubs, t-ball, badminton racquets and a basketball hoop adorned our front yard. It was exhausting learning to care for twins, yet keeping them busy meant they'd sleep at night. It continued on when our third son was born and our life revolved around providing for and nurturing our boys. All seemed well those first few years of their little lives and although it was time consuming, it was also a lot of fun. The lifestyle we had become accustomed to while working and living abroad allowed for ample leisure time within the secluded and lovely little neighborhood of other families with small children and infants.

As our sons grew their father introduced them to what I considered inappropriate and risky behaviors, yet my concerns were always met with chuckles and explanations that it was all in good fun. Once I came home to discover from the neighbor that he had actually sat our toddlers on the hood of our car while slowly driving up and down our street with music blasting. He said he was pretending it was a parade. And then there were lots of little friends coming around and playing in the streets with all the sports equipment we had. My husband created a quaint patio area with a small bonfire pit and BBQ. He thought it was all fun and games to dare the kids to hold little hot rocks from the pit or touch their skin with a hot poker as he demonstrated. They were real men if they could do this. I found out about this stunt when asking one of my sons about a little blister I found on his arm one morning. One early evening when I was home alone with the baby, the doorbell rang. There stood a police officer with the two oldest little boys. Their father had been arrested for driving under the influence while taking them to get ice cream. He was detained and the company we worked for was able to get him released and home. Then there was the jet-ski incident on a summer lake. Kids sat playing on a long dock that projected out into the water when my husband skied by at high speeds turning the jet-ski and spraying all the children. He also hit the end of the dock and a few children fell into the lake. No matter what he did orwhat happened, our sons followed their father around like the Pied Piper. He was their first hero and they worshipped him.

When we had to leave our home abroad and return to the states, life got very busy and more complicated. There was less leisure time and more work. The boys started to become involved in organized sports, playing musical instruments and making friends. There were doctor appointments and school conferences and we joined a church. We had a home to care for, big yards and pets. We looked like an All American Family. As the years progressed, even more activities would be added to our already overloaded calendars. My husband would work longer hours, and begin to spend his weekends visiting his aging parents three hours away. As the children grew older, and he progressed in his career, I took on more and more of the parenting responsibilities. He would still attend the school concerts, championship games and birthday parties. He was the loudest dad at sports playoffs, and even had a reputation of being ejected by officials for his rants.

His demeanor towards our oldest sons began to shift, however. There were power struggles and wrestling matches where he would hurt them. He would tell them again and again how much harder he worked at things when they were his age, how respectful he was toward his mother, and that they needed to step it up. He was pushing them away. All the other parents would shower my husband with praise on what amazingly funny and talented sons he had raised and how proud he must be of them, jokingly referring to him as 'Father-of-the-Year'.

~~~~~

The temporary parenting plan went into effect about six weeks after our legal separation when I had initially filed for divorce. Prior to that he had been trying to discuss visiting our sons, yet our youngest was the only one interested. My lawyer advised me not to begin any sort of schedule until the court issued the orders. Even so, I allowed him to take our youngest on weekday evenings after school and a couple of weekends. After the temporary orders went into effect, my lawyer advised me to strictly adhere to the outlined visitation schedule. So I took the family calendar and systematically documented dates and times for the one weekday evening and alternate weekends and holidays. It was a horrible feeling. He'd park in front of the house and honk. Sometimes our oldest would be home, yet they always remained indoors. I worked hard at showing my youngest son that I wanted to be cordial and kind to his father during these transitions. My husband and I had discussed this very thing when we sat on the porch that day. And so I would approach his truck, engage in small talk and send them off with a smile and a wave. My son cried that it wasn't enough time to see his dad and how could my lawyer make this happen. I realized the parental alienation had begun, although I didn't know what that even was at the time. My husband was telling our youngest son that he couldn't see him more because the lawyers and judges had decided and that I wouldn't allow it either.

Then one night shortly after that, when my husband brought our youngest home, I looked out the window and saw someone in the car with them. It was the other woman. Contrary to what we were advised while legally separated and pending divorce, he had introduced our youngest to his 'special friend' weeks after leaving his wife and home. The oldest boys happened to be outside with their high school buddies when they saw her. They stormed back into the house where one of them broke a mirror and the other punched a hole in a bedroom door. I called my husband the next day to ask him not to bring her to our house again and what the older boys had done. The next week I received a letter from my lawyer stating that visitation exchanges would need to take place in the neutral location of a grocery store parking lot as my husband had reported to his lawyer that I was making transitions difficult for him at our home. Apparently I had approached his car in a rage about the other woman and frightened them both with a tirade that all the neighbors and our sons had seen and heard.

With the continued false allegations, smear campaign and manipulation of the parenting plan, I relied more and more on the structure and boundaries within the plan. I left no room for interpretation and would not collaborate with him if he requested anything not outlined. I no longer had much control over my own schedule. My life outside of my job consisted of caring for the needs of three children and adhering to a visitation schedule that meant I had to turn down weekend trips to my family's or not accept social invitations. Whereas my husband had to give twenty-four hour notice if he was going to cancel a visit, it never happened. I'd get a call or a text a few hours before transition time or not at all. He'd end up cutting his weekday out of the schedule. He'd cancel entire weekends or call me on a Friday afternoon that he'd be two hours late, or Sunday morning that he was returning our son at noon instead of the five-o-clock evening time. I brought this madness to the attention of my lawyer and he just advised me to continue to follow the temporary parenting plan and document all these incidences. Thus began my obsession with cross-referencing my husband's behaviors with the plan's guidelines. I was outraged. I was an independent mother of three troubled boys, and going through a divorce while my husband was living the life of a bachelor in love with little to no responsibilities outside of caring for his own wants and needs.

After the divorce, and when my former husband moved three hours away, my youngest son became more and more distraught over the endless custody and visitation drama. I could feel him shutting down his emotions on Thursday nights when we'd pack his belongings into my car in preparation of me picking him up right after school in order to get on the road and make it to the transition location on time. He'd get ready and go to bed like a robot. That was his way of harboring the pain he felt in leaving his home, his neighborhood, his brothers and mother to visit his father who no longer was acknowledging any of us. On the way to the transition location, I would attempt small talk with my son, play fun music, or sing. Anything. But he knew it was forced and that I was choking back tears all the way to meet his father. On my way home I sobbed uncontrollably as I had just watched my son embrace his father after he had completely ignored my presence. I regularly would phone one of my sisters or a friend and they'd talk me home. If no one answered my calls, I would pull over on the side of the freeway and sob until I was able to drive. The first Christmas holiday exchange was excruciatingly painful as it ironically occurred at nine-o-clock in the evening on

Christmas Eve.

Time wore on and the parenting plan would continue to be manipulated. There would be an increase in late notices, cancellations, and changing the travel logistics. He used our son as his messenger. There would also be multiple texts from his cell phone on late Thursday night contradicting the one before it, until I had no idea what I was to do the following afternoon. When I'd ask for clarification I was called a stupid bitch and to figure it out. There are too many incidences to recall where I drove over dangerous mountain passes only to arrive and find him not waiting or at an alternative location that he supposedly had informed me of the previous evening. I did what the parenting plan orders outlined in situations where conflict was impacting the child. I called the dispute resolution center for help. They were wonderful in reviewing the plan with me, confirming my worries and stress, and scheduling an appointment with my former husband and me to discuss the issues. In all, he was invited to participate in mediation with me on three separate occasions. He never responded to the invitations.

I was also learning to play referee with my older sons who were taking out their repressed anger on their little brother. They referred to him as a traitor, told him to take a shower when we'd arrive home late Sunday nights because he smelled like his pig of a father. He was called Daddy's Little Angel, The Chosen One, The Gold Digger and on and on. He would come home with new clothes, very expensive shoes, sports equipment, movies and even a brand new X-Box at one point. All the while his high school brothers received nothing aside from a couple hundred bucks in a birthday card with a message asking them to help him be a better father to them. I wrote to their father asking that the extravagant gift giving stop. He replied through his lawyer that I no longer could tell him what to do or how to live his life. I sought the help of a child psychiatrist who tried to work with all three boys on sibling bonding until the oldest refused to continue to go. My life felt like hell on earth and something had to give.

When I filed a motion and declaration for a court order to show contempt, I already had over a year's worth of documented incidences. I had visited the court facilitator to schedule a hearing with intentions of asking for help from the family law courts. I was prepared. I was stronger, more confident, and had a mountain of examples that my husband was neglecting our oldest children and psychologically abusing our youngest. I also had been offered an extra hour of work each day at a good wage that my former husband would not honor on Friday night visitations. On those nights that he said no to me working an extra hour, he would show up to the transition location one hour late. So in court, I was going to talk parental and sibling alienation, and harassment toward me. I wanted justice. This had to stop.

A friend who attended court with me said afterward that I had done an amazing job. She said I looked and acted just like all the other lawyers. I didn't feel that way. Once again, and true to form, my former husband's lawyer focused on me. When I had proved his absenteeism from all of his sons' lives, I was accused of making his life so difficult when he lived here that he had no other option. Eventually I had run him out of town. When I presented documentation of mileage and gasoline and missed hours from work due to his inability to give prior notice of his change of plans, I was called a liar because he had given messages to our son whom he believed was mature enough to assume this role. When I presented the box full of returned certified mail that contained medical bills, juvenile court documents and information on college preparations there was nothing his lawyer could say except to repeat that I had run him out of town. Finally the judge stepped in and asked exactly what it was that I wanted. My documented request was asking for unnecessary travel expenses and that lost wages be reimbursed. I assumed he'd be disciplined at the court's discretion for the mistreatment of the children. All I could muster in a reply to the judge was that I wanted 'him' to stop hurting our children.

The judge discussed a few things regarding communication, asked a couple of questions and indirectly addressed a few of my concerns. She then ordered that we continue to follow the visitation schedule, reiterated that the father was to notify the mother within twenty-four hours of any cancellations, and communication was to be simple, brief and factual texts. The child was not to be used as a messenger. My motion to show just cause for contempt in not following the existing parenting plan was denied. She apologized to me that there wasn't anything else she could do to help me. The tears started to flow, and that was the last time I was inside a family law courtroom. No one was ever going to hold this monster accountable. Family law had been, and was always going to be, about legally dissolving a civil contract called marriage and dividing the property of the two persons who willingly entered that contract, including any children. I left the courthouse with my head down focusing on the ground and sidewalk in front of me so as not to see my former husband. It was crowded near the exit and I looked up in time to see his new wife and her adult daughters joyously hugging him while proclaiming they thought he was an amazing father.

Visitations continued. He kept up the same behaviors. I knew the courts would not help me, so I did my best to ignore it and focus more and more on my own healing and well being and becoming a stronger more present mother to all of my sons. This I could control. After several months of the continued visitation chaos, our youngest son went to his father's for an extended summer visit. It was on the way home from this visit that he told me he had let his dad and his wife have it. Three years of anger, disappointment and sadness had finally surfaced. He was truthful about what he felt had transpired and the pain we all had suffered because of his father's choices. He was unapologetic to his father. Once home, he seemed like a completely different child. I received a court order in the mail about two weeks later that had been prepared by my former husband's lawyer and asking for my signature. It stated that my youngest was of the age where he could now use his own discretion regarding the visitation schedule. I signed the order and he chose to never visit his father again.

> Instead of trying to gain everyone else's approval,
> you will at some point find yourself wondering
> why people can't be more like you.
> Why can't they be easy-going, kind, caring, selfless,
> accommodating, and self-aware?
> This is called self-respect.
> This is your self-worth coming from within.
> Of course it still feels good to make someone else happy,
> but now you have a much better measure
> of who deserves your light.
> And this will bring you joy for the rest of your life.
>
> ~**Peace**

Chapter Five
ON FINDING A TRIBE
People Who Cared Enough

The day I walked out of the family law courtroom for the last time, was the day that I began in earnest to make important and lasting decisions for the welfare of my children and for my own mental and physical health. I was done. I was on my own. This was a liberating move, yet I was also scared to death. I had been relying on so many people to help me make so many decisions, yet nothing was getting any better and I was feeling bad that I wasn't doing what people thought I should do. And oftentimes, each new idea or suggestion seemed to negate what someone else had just said. There were family, friends, colleagues, neighbors and support groups. It was a cacophony of deafening advice. I had to also step away from this and learn to rely on myself. I had never done that.

~~~~

Family of Origin. These are the people we usually turn to in times of need. They are always there and ready to help. Both my parents had passed away, yet I had six adult siblings and their spouses and children. They were in utter shock regarding my husband's affair and him leaving the home. They didn't know the man behind the mask because like most people they saw the Super Dad, the man of faith, and the doting husband.

My stories were met with rebuttals mixed with disbelief and confirmations that they had known all along. Like me, they started taking trips downmemory lane and analyzing events from the past and re-interpreting his most recent behaviors based on this newfound knowledge that he was a rage-a-holic and a cheater. They cared so much for my sons and me, and they were so angry with my husband. They wanted him punished, yet they had considered him to be their brother for many, many years. They were hurting, too.

I initially relied on my siblings throughout the legal separation and divorce to help me pick up the pieces of my broken life. What I appreciate now, and what I see as being the most helpful during those initial days and weeks and months of turmoil, is similar to what you see during a disaster with casualties. They became the helpers. The first responders. They showed up with groceries. They sent my sons cards or small gifts in the mail expressing their love. They helped clean and re-arrange closets and rooms where my husband's things had been. They would leave their own families and lives driving hours through the night to just sit with me or lay beside me in my bed as I sobbed uncontrollably. They had a security system installed in my home so that the kids and I would feel protected. They attended court hearings surrounding me like a protective shield from the noise and people who were continuing to hurt me. They gave me gift certificates for massages or spa visits. They never stopped asking what I needed or what they could do to make things better. They helped a shattered mother and her children feel like they did matter, they were loved and they were very special.

What my family couldn't do was help me make sense of my husband's behavior, the life we had been living, and my own mental health issues. I was so frustrated that deep inside I wasn't feeling any better. My innermost thoughts and pain were being met with affirmations that my husband was a jerk, an egomaniac and selfish. My agitated state seemed to be getting worse. I'm not sure if there was a specific event or time when I decided to redefine my relationship with my siblings as one of, well, siblings. I continued to accept their lovingkindnesses toward my sons and me, yet I stopped looking for them to help me answer the 'why' questions. They really didn't have the capabilities to do that, nor should I have expected them to act in those roles.

In-Laws. My husband's parents and siblings had been my second family for most of my adult life. Because my mother had died when I was a child, and my father was not present for most of my life before he passed away, my husband's parents were my parents, too. They referred to me as their daughter and I loved them. There were decades of holidays, birthdays, reunions and gatherings. And just life. My mother-in-law died about a year or so prior to my husband and my legal separation. My father-in-law's degenerative disease progressed rapidly after his wife died, and he passed away during our separation. As for the rest of the family members, they initially reached out to my sons and me yet it wouldn't be for long. They were all quick to take a side, support their brother in his decisions, and welcome the other woman into their world. It was unfathomable to me that these people who had once claimed me as their daughter and sister would turn away so quickly and with such vehemence.

I have since come to an understanding of what occurred and why. Like my family, they knew my husband as the perfect father, the supportive spouse, and their faithful and loving son and brother. They had rarely seen his mistreatment towards our sons and me because when we gathered, it was always under the guises of some celebration where he was always the life of the party. And because we lived overseas for so many years that they didn't really know the man I knew. The other woman presented herself as the savior to his woes, rescuing him from a very, very ill woman who was poisoning his children against him. My husband and her smear campaign against me within his family would include stories of my mental health, my raging, my alcoholism and my unavailability as a loving and committed wife. To this day I still cannot understand why they turned away from the children, however.

Eventually, one brother-in-law and his wife would turn toward their nephews and me. They had watched and listened to everything that went on during the separation, divorce and beyond. They witnessed their nephews' worlds' fall apart and began to acknowledge all I was doing to hold everything together. They began to make sense of it. They discovered the untruths. And they carefully reached out to me. My brother-in-law's acceptance of the situation while coming to painful terms with the man he started to see, was a pivotal point in my healing journey. To hear the words 'I believe you' and 'I know what you are up against' helped me embrace that I wasn't crazy. He stepped up and helped my oldest two through their difficult years of high school. He and his wife bought them clothes and athletic shoes when they needed them. They attended all of their sporting events. They came to juvenile court. They put aside their own angst and pain about what their brother had done, and reached out unconditionally to my sons and me. Like my family, they showed that we did matter. And that we were loved.

Friends. There's a country western song about knowing who your friends are. They'll drop what they are doing to get to you as quickly as they can. No explanations needed and no judgment given. They just show up. True friends, anyway. Most of the friends in my husband and my life only knew the man who attended the mutual events and parties. Just like our families, they saw him as fun loving, witty, kind and giving. When the story about what had happened began to surface, it was like a car wreck to most of them. They were shocked to hear of the accident, maybe drove to the scene and watched what unfolded in the aftermath, or heard about us on the news or from the paper. These people weren't really my friends and they would fall to the wayside eventually. I learned the hard way that telling my story to people who really didn't know the man behind the mask made me look very unwell.

Then something else began to happen. The true friends slowly began to come forward and offer support and understanding because they knew more than I thought they did. People whom I thought had seen my family as perfectly functioning hadn't seen us like that at all. Like my brother-in-law's impact on my healing, their stories were affirmations that I was not crazy. They did know the man behind the mask. These were the friends that didn't rush to the car accident. They remained in the background and as I began to recover and move forward, they offered consistent support. They truly cared. They listened without responding. They offered safe and quiet places where I could tell the story in greater detail. They found humor where I could not. They showed up with food or invited me out to coffee. They complimented me endlessly on the way I was raising my sons. And I wasn't angry at these friends for not coming forth sooner to offer help or shake some sense in to me. I wouldn't have believed them, as one of my friends told me. I was too committed to my family and my marriage.

Neighbors. I found out that no matter how private you may believe your home is, neighbors always know more than you think. I found from all sides that fights had been heard, and that my husband's treatment of me had not gone unnoticed. One neighbor lady from across the street approached me several months after my husband had left. It was the first time I had ever spoken to her since moving to the neighborhood years prior. We talked idly for a bit and then she shared what my former husband had told her once. I was not a well woman and on different medications and that it was probably best she just let me be. She apologized profusely when I told her more of the story. And on both sides of my home were elderly neighbors who would invite me over for tea often. Words of wisdom from their lives always rang true and would settle my anxiety and worries. There would be flowers from gardens on my doorstep, calls to remind me to turn on the outdoor lights, and even a backyard neighbor who turned on a floodlight one evening when I thought I had seen a prowler.

Colleagues. I learned the hard way that it really wasn't appropriate to bring my personal life to the workplace. At work, we have jobs to do. We get paid to do these jobs, and that has to be at the forefront of our actions and interactions while on the job. The car wreck scenario also fit within the workplace, yet the crowds that stood around after the wreck discussing what they saw seemed to follow me as I tried to recover from the initial shock of what had happened. Like paparazzi. So I just kept retelling the story and adding more and more detail with each new telling desperate to be believed. This only fueled the gossip and scandal. When the HR department delivered a stern reprimand regarding all of this, I had to stop entertaining people's needs to know more than they should. I only remember two colleagues who had significant impacts on my healing. One, who had gone through a horrific divorce herself years earlier, told me that there would absolutely come a day when I would be able to sing the song 'Here Comes the Sun', and on that day the world would suddenly feel different. And there was a second colleague with whom I developed a very special friendship. I would be able to rely on her for support and help, day after day. She never tired of listening to my stories or helping me think more clearly. If it hadn't been for her, I would have lost my job.

Former colleagues from our years overseas had also contacted me through social media and email. I wasn't prepared for their responses regarding my marriage and husband. It was just a matter of time, they said. It was a lengthy email from the chief executive officer who fired my husband overseas that healed my heart in ways I can't describe. It also revealed to me to what extent my husband had gone to project his own dysfunction on to me. In the email, he apologized to me for the pain that his decision caused the children and me. It was one of the most difficult decisions of his career to send a young family away from a secure lifestyle. Yet he had counseled my husband that he needed professional help for his alcohol abuse, and that his anger and rage were impacting the community and our workplace to the point that he could no longer enable his behavior. He was told to return to the states and seek out the support and help he would need to become healthy and to better care for his family. He ended the email by telling me he wasn't surprised about the direction our lives took and how it all played out in the end. He had predicted it. He cared for the children and me all those years ago, yet it was beyond his power to help us in any way other than what he did. He had a company and a community to care for as well.

~~~~~

Ultimately what I have learned from people in my life, and the various roles they have played during my healing journey, is that all the differing suggestions and contributions had a purpose in the end. It's as though I've been presented with a giant collage. From afar you see this dramatic and uniquely created wholeness, yet it's only when coming close that you can admire the thought and effort that went in to its making. What I've also learned is that it's not the quantity as much as the quality of persons that have helped me in becoming, and I have to make better choices about who I want in my life and for what reason. I need to surround myself with people who will keep me moving forward. For me, they are the people who are gentle and kind. They are the lovers. And the givers. The dreamers and truth-seekers. They look for the best in others. They encourage and build up, accept and celebrate. They know the healing powers of humor and don't confuse it with sarcasm. They don't want to know about the pain I've lived. They already sense it by looking in my eyes. They already know of it through my character and compassion and desire to help others in need. They focus on the realization that our time on earth is short, and that by living in the present, one can find happiness and joy. They want to share their light and bask in mine.

> Someday, the light will shine like a sun
> through my skin and they will say,
> 'What have you done with your life?'
> And though there are many moments
> I think I will remember, in the end
> I will be proud to say I was one of us.
>
> ~**Brian Andreas**

Chapter Six
HERE COMES THE SUN
Recovery and Beyond

I loved him with all of my heart for most of my life. I was loyal to our marriage, our family and our life to a fault. But somewhere along the way I disappeared. I ceased to exist outside the confines of an abusive relationship. I became responsible for his happiness and maintaining peace within our world. Deep inside I lived in fear that without him I would not be able to survive. I saw no way out. When he left, I did not know how to exist. People would talk about a fresh start, a new life, doing things for myself and how happy I was going to be. None of this made any sense. I just wanted my husband back. I wanted our sons' father to be present in their lives. And so for a very long time I lived in a limbo state. I couldn't go back and I couldn't move forward. I was suspended in the here and now consumed with all the little disasters that were happening around me. I was so worn down and so tired. I felt apathy toward everything, and I truly believed my life was slipping away.

One of the true friends who came forth sat me down one day to share the analogy of an airplane emergency. To get my attention, she focused on my children. Our plane was going down and without really thinking, I put on their oxygen masks first. Their masks kept falling off or getting tangled and they were in a panic mode without me. I wasn't even letting the cabin crew help or listening to them urging me to put on my own mask. I would soon be losing consciousness and not be able to care for my children at all if I didn't take care of myself and allow others to help me with the children. That simple analogy was all it took to help me begin to see things different and start to move forward. At this point, some sort of 'will to live' kicked in. It was self-preservation, and I am confident that a higher power lifted me up and held on to me. There is no human explanation for how my heart and mind and soul rallied out of the darkest despair I had ever experienced.

I had already been attending the twelve-step support group and women's abuse group. Both of these were very helpful, yet they focused on my husband's behaviors and the impact he had had on my life for so long. I started to wonder more about me. I knew I had to re-direct my efforts toward self-care so I paid more attention to diet and sleep. For starters, my physical body was in shambles. I had lived off of adrenaline for so long, and was in such a chronic state of hyper-vigilance, that I was exhausted. I had lost too much weight during the divorce. I had been eating horribly and self-medicating with alcohol and over-the-counter sleeping aids. My physical recovery started when I began to eat better. Even if I wasn't hungry, I ate nutritious meals. I drank a lot of water and hot tea. This was the fuel I needed to take bigger steps in my healing journey.

Next, I focused on sleep. I knew the short and long term effects of sleep deprivation from my years of traveling abroad and from raising children. I was experiencing memory loss, depression and irritability. I was having difficulty falling asleep in the evening, couldn't get out of bed in the morning and was unable to enjoy an afternoon nap. I decided to overhaul my bedroom. I purchased soft sheets, a new comforter, curtains and a soothing paint color. I purchased a white noise fan. And I treated my bedroom as if it were a cocoon. I would enter my cocoon having bathed and in a relaxed state, shut the door, turn on the noise fan and wrap myself up like a caterpillar. I found that gently rocking myself helped in falling asleep. I attempted to quiet my thoughts by remembering that sleep had a purpose and everything that was going on outside of my cocoon was going to happen with or without me. Within a few weeks of restructuring my diet and sleep habits, I felt much, much better.

Exercise and getting out of the house was also important. I had always been very active and conscious about my looks. I was a runner at one time. I had gym memberships for aerobics and weight training. This type of exercise proved to be too much during my recovery. Along with too many people and the bright lights, the blasting music and dropped weights kept me on edge. I found myself angry in the gym. I couldn't concentrate and it wasn't helping. So I sought out gentler exercise. I began taking long walks through pretty neighborhoods and parks. I learned to enjoy swimming for a few months with the quiet, rhythmic motions of gliding through the water. Finally, and at the suggestion of a friend, I tried yoga. It met all of my needs and I learned to meditate and focus which in turn helped me to re-direct my thoughts.

How was I going to untie all the knots in my brain? I was so tangled up within my husband's persona that I didn't know where he ended and where I started. I was enmeshed in his dysfunction. I began working with a personal therapist on my marriage and divorce. Nothing else. I could have filled those hourly sessions with many, many other issues. But I didn't. It was hard work. Emotional and heartfelt work. But she was so compassionate and always there for me. I felt safe almost immediately and I knew she knew there was no 'snapping out of it'. I learned about trauma bonding and boundaries. I was able to confront flashbacks and memories triggered through songs, foods or places. I became moreand more confident and unafraid in confronting conflict generated by the legal system during my separation and divorce. I also began to identify the beauty inside that had been hidden away for so very long. I re-discovered my gifts and talents and how I could share them with others. I addressed my resistance to anything that pushed me further along than I wanted to go. I instinctively knew that I wanted more than anything to reclaim myself and to live an authentic life free from the pain and angst that had become my constant companions.

My faith had taken a back seat for some time and that was nagging at me as I began to feel better physically and emotionally. The family that once attended mass every Sunday no longer filled a particular pew. My older sons stopped going, and my youngest was resistant to attend. I didn't push any of them, as I had stopped too. I was angry with God. Instead of praying for help, I blamed him for everything that had happened. I had been a good wife, a wonderful mother and a kind neighbor. I had always tried to live by the Golden Rule, yet look at my life now. When I finally returned to church one Sunday, I sobbed through the entire mass on my knees. People let me be for the most part, yet I remember being hugged, and somebody holding my hand. Holiday masses were especially painful. But I kept going. And I kept crying.

I also began to speak to my priest on a consistent basis and he helped me tremendously in accepting the human condition, God's participation in it, and finding a spirituality that helps one to see the other side of life's hard knocks. He helped me to finally be able to do something that allowed me to set aside, for the better, the false hope I was holding on to that my husband would come back to our children and me. He helped me to forgive. It didn't mean that who he was or what he did was acceptable or would ever be forgotten. I still had to exercise boundaries and caution where he was concerned. What it meant was that he was incapable of being the kind of husband I needed and the kind of father that my sons deserved. He couldn't be that man. I could no longer be consumed with thoughts and dreams that he would return and pay me what I was owed. He didn't have it to pay. And so I forgave him of those debts. I set him free. And in doing that, I was able to forgive myself for the pain I believed I caused to our children, to him and to me in trying so hard to collect the debts.

I began to feel myself detaching from obessive thoughts about my former husband's influence on my children and me. I could no longer care. It was killing me. I also felt a resolve within that if the children did indeed end up returning to their father, or if they were to display psychopathic tendencies themselves, there would be little to nothing I could do to stop it. I pictured what my life would look like without my children, and how I would continue to live and function. I was determined to continue to be a good and loving mother, but I had to focus on myself now. It was during this fierce time of self protection and healing that my children's recovery was most noticeable. They saw me becoming healthier, and they gravitated more toward me and further from him.

I found myself looking at people differently. I started to see the behaviors of my family, friends and colleagues from other angles. I had always wanted to be accepted so badly that I allowed people to mistreat me. And when they mistreated me, I had fallen right into the victim role. It was when I found a very special online abuse recovery forum that my healing progressed significantly in how I saw myself and others. It was moderated closely through a small and very dedicated group of abuse survivors. I joined as an anonymous member and began to share my stories with other anonymous members in like situations and at various points in their healing journeys. There was no end to the acceptance, understanding and encouragement I found. There was always someone to talk to and share with, day or night, and they became my lifeline during a very lonely and vulnerable time. The pieces of my life began to make sense.

I soon found myself interacting with others in the real world in healthier ways. I was able to express what I needed and wanted from others. I began to identify unhealthy behaviors and toxic personalities and developed skills in dealing with people in ways that kept me safe and at peace, including my former husband with whom I had a court mandated relationship due to shared custody. My older sons had lived a life of being exposed to domestic abuse. They never witnessed mature and healthy adult love between their parents. And so when their father left, they took up where he left off with the verbal abuse toward me, the anger and rage, and disrespect. I had to apply newly acquired relationship skills with them, too, and teach them that I would not tolerate that kind of treatment. While learning to interact with people, I started to feel better about myself. I was learning to love myself. And for what seemed like the first time in my life, I started to feel comfortable in my own skin.

I also turned my focus to my financial recovery. Little by little, child support decreased and bills increased. Whereas I once had enough money to live a very comfortable life, I was now living paycheck-to-paycheck, cutting back on anything not necessary, and obsessing over budgets. Every cent counted. I re-financed my home and paid my former husband the divorce settlement, even though he was now independently wealthy. I cleaned out closets and rooms and had yard sales. I began shopping with coupons and at wholesale stores. I stopped buying trunk loads of beautiful flower baskets in the spring for my front porch and back patio. When my sons and I traveled for sports or school events, we stayed in hotels with no-star ratings as opposed to the resorts we had become accustomed to while living and traveling abroad. I sold jewelry and our family car. I set up payment plans with all of my sons' doctors for the continued accumulation of medical co-pays that their father stopped paying once the oldest turned eighteen.

~~~~~

How long does it take to rebuild a life impacted by a psychopath? When do you know that it's over and you have arrived to the magic place? Every answer is different, and that's the ultimate challenge for us parents who have had children with a toxic person. Our stories may be eerily similar, but our healing journeys are unique. For most of my life I was addicted to drama and conflict. I learned to expect it, and if it wasn't there, I created it. I missed a lot of life by living like that. What I believe at this moment is that I will always be traveling a road of personal discovery and growth. It's just who I am. I seek quiet now. I live one day at a time, and I make an effort to be conscious and aware of the life around me. I try to move through each day more slowly and with purpose. I listen more and talk less. I feel good. I feel strong. I bounce back more quickly from setbacks and inevitable disappointments. I am hopeful going forth. Hopeful for my sons and for me. Hopeful that the 'us' we have become will continue to evolve into a renewed and stronger family. Hopeful that the work I've done in removing myself from a life of sorrow and darkness will keep me standing in the sun.

I do acknowledge that my sons may one day reach out to their father. They may want to see him or talk to him at least. There will be nothing I can do. I can only pray that after all we have been through, and all we have grown to be together, that they will be able to see his sickness and keep their boundaries in place in whatever kind of relationship they choose to have with him.

Today I look at the psychopath in my life as another life event that was not planned or expected. Like natural disasters, deaths, disease, or any other difficult human experience, psychopathic abuse happened. It is truly what I have done with the experience that has determined the direction my life, and the lives of my children, will take.

> Be soft. Do not let the world make you hard.
> Do not let the pain make you hate.
> Do not let the bitterness steal your sweetness.
> Take pride that even though the rest of the world may disagree,
> you still believe it to be a beautiful place.
>
> ~Kurt Vonnegut

AFTERWARD
When All is Said and Done

Shortly before this book went to print, I was literally on my way out the door to spend a long weekend with my siblings two hours away. It was my fiftieth birthday. A milestone. And I felt very happy, which was surprising being that I had dreaded the arrival of 'that birthday' for a long time. And there she stood at the end of my driveway. A currier was serving me papers summoning me to appear in Superior Court for child support modification.

The very first thought that came to mind was that being served on this day was no coincidence. Covert bullying had been a pattern of my former husband's behaviors throughout the past several years. It had almost become comical. His wedding announcement to the other woman would appear in the local paper on the anniversary date that he left the family home. I'd receive, on what would have been our twenty-fifth wedding anniversary, a text stating I was a sad, pathetic, lonely and unhappy woman. One Mother's Day he would bring our youngest son home six hours late from his visitation having missed our family BBQ and visiting relatives. On New Year's Day he would make me drive hours out of my way to retrieve my youngest son per the parenting plan transition location guidelines, when he knew I was a mere forty-five minute drive from his home tending to my older son who had just moved in to his first college apartment. And on and on and on.

I went back into the house and read through the stack of legal documents. Most significantly, he had resigned from his six figure corporate job he had taken three years prior and was now planning on becoming a farmer. His projected monthly income as a farmer would mean my current child support would be reduced by eighty percent. Four letters accompanied his motion, all written by various women in his life. His wife. Two colleagues. The human resources office. Each described him as a wonderful, hardworking and dedicated corporate executive, struggling with the reality of leaving a professional career he had worked so diligently at over the years. His wife's letter added that she was no longer able to care for the farm on her own, and needed his help in carrying out her dying father-in-law's wishes. A fifth letter was from his primary physician. He could not disclose the diagnoses or medications, yet was recommending my former husband resign from his professional career due to significant and chronic stress impacting his physical health. Farming would be an appropriate career solution.

The underlying sentiment that focused on his health and wellness and personal happiness in all of these letters was almost identical to the disclosures from our divorce documents, including his justifications for bringing another woman into our marriage. So now it's his high-powered career to blame for his failing health as opposed to his deranged, depressed, and unavailable wife. In addition to the child support reduction, I would have to add all three sons to my medical insurance plan since their father couldn't afford to insure them, himself, and his wife on a farmer's income. This would mean a pay deduction for me in covering the family plan premium.

So many thoughts were running through my head. I was supposed to be driving down the freeway on a sunny May morning, listening to tunes and enjoying my coffee in anticipation of a celebration weekend. Yet here I sat in my dining room struggling with a jumbled mess of mixed emotions. On one hand I was frightened to death that I wasn't going to be able to keep the family home any longer. On the other hand I felt an overwhelming peace that I was that much closer to being completely free of this man. And I knew him so well. Why was I even surprised at all about these documents, and being served on my birthday no less?

I could easily sit down and write a scathing response. I knew he was not reporting income to the IRS from various projects on the farm. I knew of the balances of his savings that an older sibling was hiding in multiple accounts. I knew the long-term plans he had for increased income with the with the farmland, and that these plans had been put into place and nurtured for decades, and while his father was alive and tending to the land himself. I knew how he would manipulate his taxes to paint a picture of a poor farmer barely surviving off of the land. I knew he was a jack-of-all-trades and kept the home, land and outer buildings in pristine condition while successfully working with the county for property tax reductions. I knew of the acreage and the endless offers from various companies to sell off small parcels for significant amounts of money that would allow him to live comfortably for the rest of his life. I knew all of this because I was a part of his family and privy to the workings of their farm and estate for almost thirty years.

But at what expense to my own mental and physical health would it cost me to prove he was a lying, manipulating cheat? I had already consulted with property and estate attorneys a year ago predicting his plan. It would cost me up to ten thousand dollars, I was told, to prove all of what I knew, and then it would be a crapshoot whether or not a judge would rule in my favor. If a judge did order him to continue to pay the current child support and provide medical insurance for the children, I would most likely end up diverting most of these monies toward the attorney fees anyway. And even though I was wrestling with the angst and frustration of the situation, I knew in my heart of hearts what this new motion ultimately signified. The day had finally come where there was next to nothing left for him to take from me. Maybe I should look at this summons as a birthday gift instead.

I set down the papers and phoned his lawyer's office. I had rehearsed this response in my mind many times. My conversation with the paralegal lasted all but two minutes. I informed her I had received the summons and there would be no rebuttal from me. Please draw up the final orders indicating I agree to the decrease of child support. Please document that the mother will be providing medical insurance for all three boys. And, in addition, please ask my former husband if he would consider giving me sole custody of our minor son relinquishing him from all financial responsibilities. I wished her a good weekend and hung up.

I took just a moment to entertain my former husband's response to my acknowledgement of his motions. Would there be a sinister grin? Would he claim victory? Would he share with all the doting females in his life that my response meant he finally taught me never to cross him again? I'll never really know. In the end, when all is said and done, my relationship with the psychopath I married, and with whom I have three children, has come down to one thing. My reactions to his behaviors. It has always been, and will continue to be, my reactions that hold the power. Until the day when I can claim complete freedom.

Made in the USA
Lexington, KY
14 May 2015